Especially for

....

From

....

Date

....

Christmas REMEMBERED

A Holiday Memory Journal
for Families

JOANNE SIMMONS

BARBOUR BOOKS
An Imprint of Barbour Publishing, Inc.

Introduction

But Mary treasured up all these things
and pondered them in her heart.
LUKE 2:19 NIV

So many miraculous events comprised the birth of Jesus Christ. So many characters played important roles. And the Bible says Mary, who was just a humble virgin girl called to carry the hope of the world, "treasured up all these things and pondered them in her heart." And because these things that Mary pondered were recorded in the living and active Word of God, we have an entire season to celebrate that God came near; He is Immanuel, God with us.

Each year as you celebrate our Savior's birth, what events, what characters, what traditions, what gifts do *you* want to remember most? Don't let them escape you in all the happy hubbub. Like Mary, you can treasure them up. Simply turn the page and begin writing down all the precious moments of your holiday festivities.

In this journal you'll find questions and prompts to share your memories and musings of the Christmas season, and you'll find space to consider similar memories of Christmas past and related hopes for Christmas future, too—a bit like Charles Dickens required of Ebenezer Scrooge! Then ponder and treasure your records and reflections for years to come and generations more.

The Songs and Stories of the Season

Songs and stories seem to be the official herald of the season. When radio stations and shopping centers begin playing Christmas music, and TV channels begin airing the holiday specials, commercials, shows, and movies, we know for sure that Christmas is upon us. Whether you are a person who cringes when the music starts in early November—or you cheerfully crank up the radio—you likely have favorite songs you love to sing and stories you must read and favorite movies you must watch each year—and maybe even ones you love to hate because they're so overdone.

Whatever your thoughts on the best calendar date for Christmas stories and songs to begin and end, rejoice that while the holiday has certainly been secularized, there is still such spiritual depth to the season and a special softness to people's hearts for hearing God's Word. More so at Christmastime than any other season, the message of Jesus Christ and all the love and hope He offers is proclaimed through song and story in public and unlikely places!

The LORD has made known his salvation;
 he has revealed his righteousness
 in the sight of the nations.
He has remembered his steadfast love
 and faithfulness to the house of Israel.
All the ends of the earth have seen
 the salvation of our God.
Make a joyful noise to the LORD, all the earth;
 break forth into joyous song and sing praises!
Sing praises to the LORD with the lyre,
 with the lyre and the sound of melody!
With trumpets and the sound of the horn
 make a joyful noise before the King, the LORD!

PSALM 98:2–6 ESV

Our traditions for reading the Bible together as family at Christmas include...

Our favorite traditional Christmas carols are. . .

*O*ur favorite holiday albums/songs from popular music artists are...

Our favorite stories and books to read at Christmastime are. . .

The very best, must-watch Christmas movies are...

Our favorite Christmas TV shows are. . .

We know Christmas has officially come to our home when. . .

The Christmas songs that best bring our hearts fully into worship are. . .

Musical or theatrical Christmas productions we have been involved in:

....

....

....

....

....

....

....

....

....

....

....

....

....

....

....

....

....

....

....

....

....

....

....

....

....

....

The Christmas songs we find stuck in our heads most often are...

*S*pecial performances (like The Nutcracker or a Christmas cantata) that we attend:

The Grinch Award in our family is given to _____ because. . .

The Christmas Cheer Award in our family is given to _____ because. . .

Our favorite movie version of A Christmas Carol *is _____ because. . .*

*R*ecord "misheard" Christmas song lyrics that members of your family sing or have sung in the past:

....
....
....
....
....
....
....
....
....
....
....
....
....
....
....
....
....
....
....
....
....
....
....
....
....
....

Special Christmas concert or solo memories:

What Christmas song would you not mind if you never heard again?

Special memories of Christmas caroling:

Tinsel and Trimmings

Aside from a star, there were no decorations on that miraculous night Jesus was born. But oh, what a spectacular star it was that led wise men from afar to worship Him! And oh, what fun to let that star inspire us to deck the halls each Christmas season with tinsel and all the trimmings! Do you go all out or keep things simple? Cut your own real tree or haul the artificial one down from the attic? Decorate with outdoor lights or just don't bother? Use particular colors and formal themes or have a casual assortment of nostalgic items? Whatever your holiday style, jot down the details simply for the joy of remembering them—and rejoice, especially that the season to celebrate our Savior's birth inspires so much delightful decor.

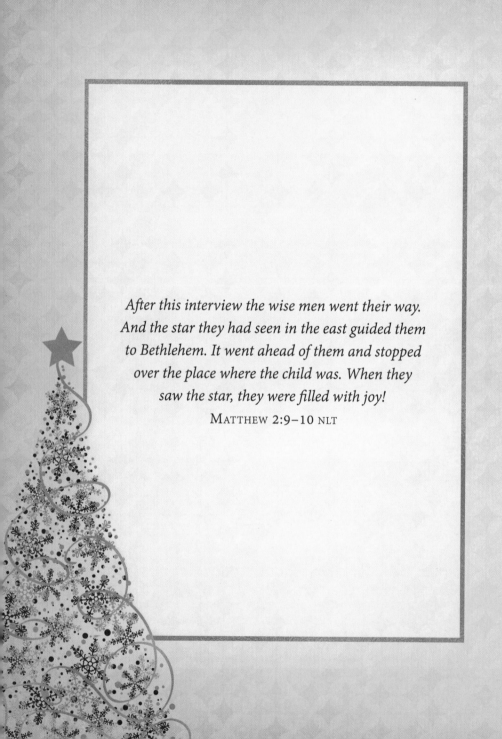

After this interview the wise men went their way. And the star they had seen in the east guided them to Bethlehem. It went ahead of them and stopped over the place where the child was. When they saw the star, they were filled with joy!

MATTHEW 2:9–10 NLT

*O*ur holiday decorating traditions:

New additions to our indoor decorations include. . .

Describe your Nativity scene(s) and what makes it/them special:

All about our Christmas tree:

What is your family's favorite type of Christmas tree? (Douglas Fir, Frasier Fir, artificial, etc.) Are there conflicting opinions about what makes the best Christmas tree?

When do you put up your Christmas tree? Do you have specific tree trimming traditions?

What is your Christmas tree's theme? Is it a hodgepodge of heartwarming, memorable ornaments or a specific look you're going for?

$\mathcal{D}$escribe your tree in detail. What makes it special to each member of your family?

Do you put up more than one Christmas tree in your home? Why and where?

List each family member's favorite heirloom ornaments or decorations. What are the stories behind them?

Describe a time when a beloved ornament or decoration broke:

Our tree topper is. . .

Describe your stockings and any traditions associated with them:

How do you decorate the outside of your home?

*O*ur favorite special lights/decoration exhibits to visit are. . .

Do you participate in any lighting or decorating contests? Describe the experience:

Describe and record the year that your family receives (or has received) new ornaments from friends and family:

_____

_____

_____

_____

_____

_____

_____

_____

_____

_____

_____

_____

_____

_____

_____

_____

_____

_____

_____

_____

_____

_____

_____

_____

_____

_____

Describe special handmade ornaments and the story behind them:

Describe any edible decorations you make every year (gingerbread houses, popcorn strings, etc.):

The decoration that is most controversial in our home is. . .

Festive Feasting

Cookies and candy, traditional treats, loved ones gathered around the table for a festive feast. . . Christmastime certainly features a bevy of beloved foods. Be sure to record those extra-special, top-secret family recipes and pass them on to each new generation. The preparation is just as fun as the feasting itself! What warms the heart more than baking goodies with Grandma or roasting chestnuts on an open fire with dear old Dad?

Whatever your holiday table holds, receive it with gratitude to the heavenly Father from whom all blessings flow—and "whether you eat or drink, or whatever you do, do all to the glory of God" (1 Corinthians 10:31 ESV).

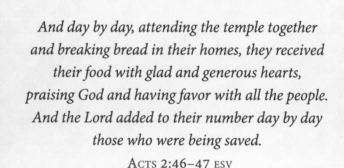

*And day by day, attending the temple together
and breaking bread in their homes, they received
their food with glad and generous hearts,
praising God and having favor with all the people.
And the Lord added to their number day by day
those who were being saved.*

ACTS 2:46–47 ESV

Our must-have traditional treats each year are. . . (Be sure to record the recipe!)

Our favorite thing to smell as it cooks or bakes is. . . (What special memories accompany that smell?)

Describe your experiences with a cookie exchange/swap. What cookies did you make? What were your favorites you collected?

Describe cookie trays from neighbors, coworkers, or friends. Whose trays does your family look forward to every year?

We tried these new recipes:

These new recipes were a big hit:

These new recipes were not so good:

These new recipes were a gigantic disaster:

*W*hat food is the main-dish star of your Christmas feast? Traditional turkey or ham or something nontraditional? Why do you make what you make?

*W*hat memorable mishaps occurred during holiday cooking and baking?

Our favorite holiday beverages are...

*W*here and when did you feast? With whom?

Describe a time when you couldn't have your "normal" Christmas feast. What happened?

The extravagant or ethnic foods we eat at Christmastime are. . .

The perfect Christmas feast menu, according to each family member, includes. . .

Describe special dishes (fine china, crystal) that you use for Christmas dinner:

Describe your Christmas centerpiece:

Describe special snacks your family eats only during the holiday season:

What is the strangest Christmas food, according to each family member?

Who are the chefs and who are the consumers in your family? What dish does each chef specialize in?

Paper and Presents, Wonder and Wishes

We love because God first loved us (1 John 4:19), and we give because He gives to us. Scripture asks, "You parents—if your children ask for a loaf of bread, do you give them a stone instead? Or if they ask for a fish, do you give them a snake? Of course not! So if you sinful people know how to give good gifts to your children, how much more will your heavenly Father give good gifts to those who ask him" (Matthew 7:9–11 NLT). And has there ever been a better gift than the one He gave us by coming as a baby to live and walk among us and then conquer death as our hope and salvation?

The wise men came from afar to worship the Holy Child and offer Him gifts, and we celebrate that gift-giving with presents of our own to one another. It's quite a challenge to not let materialism commandeer our Christmas, but by diligently focusing on Jesus and asking for God's wisdom while shopping and spending, we can rejoice in the blessings of both giving and receiving.

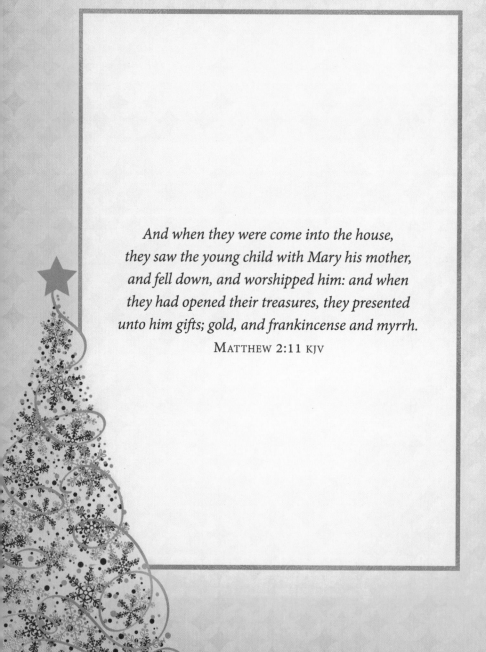

And when they were come into the house,
they saw the young child with Mary his mother,
and fell down, and worshipped him: and when
they had opened their treasures, they presented
unto him gifts; gold, and frankincense and myrrh.

MATTHEW 2:11 KJV

*W*hat type of Christmas shopper are you? Do you shop all year, at the last moment, or somewhere in between those extremes?

_____

_____

_____

_____

_____

_____

_____

_____

_____

_____

_____

_____

_____

_____

_____

_____

_____

_____

_____

_____

_____

Family and friends on our Christmas list this year are. . .

What kinds of gifts do you exchange with neighbors?

*O*ther than close family, friends, and neighbors, to whom do you give gifts or tokens of appreciation each year?

*W*hat are your favorite stores to shop for gifts? Do you shop online, in traditional stores, or some of both?

Black Friday shopping is. . .

What homemade gifts have you or your family made for others?

What homemade gifts have you and your family received?

*W*hat special gifts have your furry family members received?

Has anyone ever peeked at presents before Christmas? Describe what happened:

$\mathcal{W}$hat family traditions do you have for gift-wrapping time? Who is the best wrapper? Whose skills are a little lacking (but still festive)?

When do Christmas presents appear under the tree? Do you have family rules about touching or shaking or guessing?

Do you have Christmas stocking traditions? Are stocking gifts wrapped or unwrapped? Do stockings come first or last?

What gifts are each family member most excited to give?

Record each person's wish list here:

What are your traditions and fun stories surrounding Santa Claus and presents each year?

Our favorite childhood gifts were. . .

What is a gift each person received that has surprised him or her the most?

$\mathcal{S}$hare a regifting memory:

If money were no issue, and you could choose only one item each, what would you give each person in your immediate family for Christmas and why?

Mistletoe and Merriment: The Celebrations of the Season

Who looks forward to the Christmas season more than a young child? Children are filled with sheer wonder and delight for everything from the glowing lights on the tree to magical tales of Santa Claus to the simple sweetness of a candy cane.

No matter our age, let's hold fast to that kind of enthusiastic joy and zeal for even the simplest amusement of the season. For the source of our joy is never in the amusement itself but in the very reason we celebrate Christmas—a Savior born to rescue us all from our sin and trials and live for eternity with Him in perfect paradise. No matter our current circumstances, may that deep, abiding joy motivate all our merrymaking of the season!

In all this you greatly rejoice, though now for a little while you may have had to suffer grief in all kinds of trials. These have come so that the proven genuineness of your faith—of greater worth than gold, which perishes even though refined by fire—may result in praise, glory and honor when Jesus Christ is revealed. Though you have not seen him, you love him; and even though you do not see him now, you believe in him and are filled with an inexpressible and glorious joy, for you are receiving the end result of your faith, the salvation of your souls.

1 PETER 1:6–9 NIV

Do you send and receive Christmas cards? Who are your recipients and senders?

Record memories from a photo shoot for family Christmas photos:

Do you take the kids to see Santa? What are your most memorable experiences?

What special parties do you attend at Christmastime?

Do you dress up formally for a particular occasion? What is each family member wearing this year?

Our favorite games to play at Christmastime are. . .

*O*ur favorite crafts to do at Christmastime are. . .

*W*rite about Christmas parades or tree-lighting ceremonies that your family watches or participates in:

Describe your ugliest Christmas sweaters:

The funniest white elephant gift I ever received was...

The funniest white elephant gift I ever gave was...

$\mathcal{D}$escribe a time that someone in your family participated in a Secret Santa exchange:

Describe some cold-weather outdoor memories (sledding, skiing, skating, playing in the snow, etc.):

What does each member of your family say is the very best thing about Christmas?

Fun with Family and Friends

There seems to be an extraordinary kind of fellowship with one another at Christmastime, especially among believers. Get-togethers feel so grand, whether they are lavish parties or simple gatherings, because of the joy, the hope, and the peace that sparkles among us like at no other time of the year. Family and friends might travel far, or all your loved ones might be local. Or are you the one who travels far? Whatever the case, treasure the memories, write down whom you spent the season with, and note the highlights of your time together.

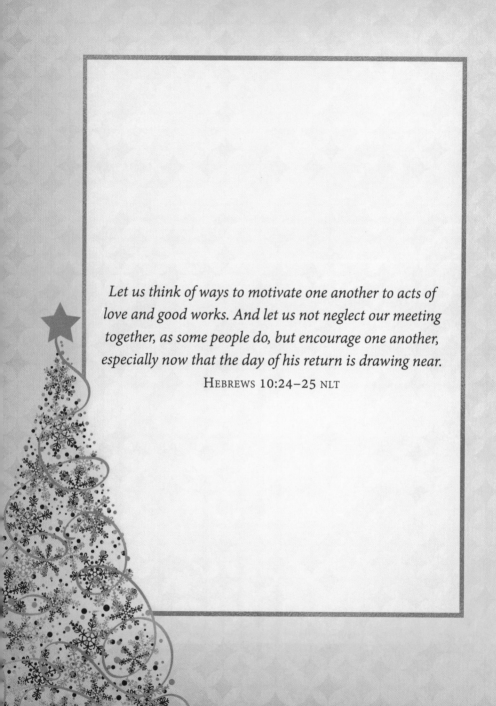

Let us think of ways to motivate one another to acts of love and good works. And let us not neglect our meeting together, as some people do, but encourage one another, especially now that the day of his return is drawing near.

HEBREWS 10:24–25 NLT

Keep a list of all the family and friends whom you visit with during Christmastime, either this year or in years past:

Where does your family travel to at Christmas?

Do you host overnight guests? Who and for how long?

*W*hat is the biggest challenge of hosting overnight guests?

*W*hat is the biggest blessing of hosting overnight guests?

Describe family Christmas pajama traditions:

A typical conversation around the Christmas dinner table with family and friends goes something like this:

Describe your experience with trying to get a group family photo:

Does your family celebrate holiday traditions from other countries or cultures? What special foods, decorations, or activities does that include?

If your whole family could go anywhere in the world for a Christmas vacation, where would you go and what would you do?

Christmas past: Our favorite memories of fun with family and friends from the past are. . .

Christmas future: Our hopes and goals for fun with family and friends in the future are. . .

Holiday Hope: The True Meaning

With such hustle and bustle overwhelming the season these days, it sometimes feels impossible to just relax and relish the season for its true meaning of hope—hope personified in the life of a baby boy, God becoming human in order to relate to us and eventually offer a way to save us from the sin that hijacked His original design for people to commune with Him, our holy Creator.

So at Christmas, be purposeful in regularly stepping away from the secularization of the season to draw near to God so that He will draw near to you (James 4:8). Choose holiday activities that focus on Jesus and sharing His love, and set aside daily devotion time to simply be still (Psalm 46:10) before God and let Him remind you of His great delight in you and what treasure you have to look forward to in heaven with Him someday, all because He first came near us at Christmastime.

"Behold, the virgin shall conceive and bear a son,
and they shall call his name Immanuel"
(which means, God with us).

MATTHEW 1:23 ESV

*O*ur Advent traditions include. . .

*W*hat live Nativity productions or special concerts (such as Handel's Messiah) do you attend to help you focus on the reason for the season?

Do you have a birthday party for Jesus? Describe it:

*W*hat are each family member's favorite scriptures about the birth of Jesus Christ?

*W*rite about your experiences ringing Salvation Army bells:

In what ways does your family give to those in need during Christmastime?

In what ways does your family serve others during Christmastime?

In what ways does your family spread cheer and hope during the Christmas season?

If you could give just one gift to every child in the world, what would it be? Record each family member's response:

....

....

....

....

....

....

....

....

....

....

....

....

....

....

....

....

....

....

....

....

....

....

Describe how you feel when you are blessing others during the Christmas season:

What is each family member most thankful for?

Describe a Christmas miracle you've witnessed:

*W*hat does each family member love most about church at Christmastime?

Describe a time when Christmas became real to your family:

Christmas past: Our favorite memories of holiday hope in the past are...

Christmas future: Our hopes and goals for holiday hope in the future are. . .

The Main Events:
Christmas Eve and Christmas Day

For children, the days seem to drag toward Christmas Eve and Christmas morning with an excruciating wait for the culmination of their yearlong dreams of presents stacked under a Christmas tree. But for adults, every year the days seem to slide faster, as if down a snowy hill, until the main events are upon us in barely the twinkle of Santa's eye. So, all the more reason to write down the details lest we forget them as the season rushes past. Normally, Christmas Eve and Christmas Day hold the main events of festive feasts and gift exchanging, but whatever day of December holds your biggest and best celebration, use the quiet times when all is said and done to record and remember those precious times together.

And the angel said to them, "Fear not, for behold,
I bring you good news of great joy that will be for all
the people. For unto you is born this day in the city
of David a Savior, who is Christ the Lord."

LUKE 2:10–11 ESV

Describe the church services your family attends on Christmas Eve or Christmas Day:

Do you host family Christmas celebrations on Christmas Eve or Christmas Day or go elsewhere?

What are your family's Christmas Eve Santa Claus traditions?

Do you open any presents on Christmas Eve?

*W*hat meals or special treats are only for Christmas Eve?

What time does the family finally go to bed on Christmas Eve?

Our idea of a perfect Christmas Eve is. . .

Who is the first person to wake on Christmas morning? What is the earliest someone has gotten up?

What is the traditional order of events on Christmas morning?

Describe your typical Christmas breakfast:

Does everyone get dressed first or stay in pajamas on Christmas morning?

*W*hat are your gift-giving traditions? Does everyone take turns opening gifts, or is it chaos around the Christmas tree?

Do you dress up or go casual for Christmas dinner?

*W*ho does most of the cooking for Christmas?

$\mathcal{D}$escribe a time that your family traveled to celebrate Christmas in a faraway place:

Describe a Christmas travel nightmare your family has experienced:

If there is no snow on Christmas, we feel. . .

*W*rite about one of your family's most meaningful Christmas traditions. Why is it so important to you?

Christmas past: Our favorite memories of the "main events" in the past are. . .

....
....
....
....
....
....
....
....
....
....
....
....
....
....
....
....
....
....
....
....
....
....
....
....
....

Christmas future: Our hopes and goals for the "main events" in the future are. . .

Ringing in the New Year

Parties and celebrations, especially if you celebrate the traditional Twelve Days of Christmas beginning on December 25 and ending on January 6, continue right on through New Year's Eve and New Year's Day. The end of the year marks a time to reflect and a time to look ahead, to start fresh as the calendar changes over. Be mindful that with each new day and new year that passes, we step closer and closer to the day when Christ, who is the ultimate Creator of all things new, will come again. His return will mark the beginning of a whole new era for all who believe in Him—an era that lasts for eternity in heaven!

Meanwhile, as we wait for His glorious return, reflect on the years that are past, have hope for the years that are to come, and ask God to show you His good plans for Your life and how best to fulfill them each day.

Then I saw a new heaven and a new earth, for the first heaven and the first earth had passed away, and the sea was no more. And I saw the holy city, new Jerusalem, coming down out of heaven from God, prepared as a bride adorned for her husband. And I heard a loud voice from the throne saying, "Behold, the dwelling place of God is with man. He will dwell with them, and they will be his people, and God himself will be with them as their God. He will wipe away every tear from their eyes, and death shall be no more, neither shall there be mourning, nor crying, nor pain anymore, for the former things have passed away." And he who was seated on the throne said, "Behold, I am making all things new."

REVELATION 21:1–5 ESV

What are your family's New Year's Eve traditions?

What are your family's New Year's Day traditions?

*W*hat are some favorite foods and recipes for New Year celebrations?

Describe a New Year's party that you hosted:

What is one thing each family member is looking forward to most about the new year?

What will you miss most from the last year?

*L*ist each family member's New Year's resolutions:

List resolutions from past years that have been successful:

The family members who definitely can stay up till midnight are...

The family members who definitely can't stay up till midnight are. . .

Describe your family's favorite festive New Year's Eve party favors:

Our favorite games to play during New Year celebrations are. . .

*R*ecord a prayer for your family for the new year here:

Our favorite memories of ringing in the new year are. . .

Our hopes and goals for ringing in the new year in the future are...

Our Family Memories: